Children, Children!

a ministry without boundaries

Dorlis Brown Glass

DISCIPLESHIP RESOURCES
MATERIALS FOR GROWTH IN CHRISTIAN FAITH AND LIFE

Photographs courtesy of "Focus '85", National Conference on Ministry with Children, Nashville, Tennessee, July 29-August 2, 1985.

ISBN 0-88177-033-7

Library of Congress Catalog Card No. 86-50509

Contents

Foreword

"Life with our boys is like going down the rapids on an air mattress . . . forever!"

Years ago my sister-in-law shared this view of family life with me. Her statement took on new meaning as our own children grew. Sometimes recalling her words brought laughter, sometimes tears.

Zipping down white water rapids can be exciting and adventurous. There are moments of danger, risk, fear. There are quiet times when you seem to be buoyed up by the river's flow and by the beauty around you. Then perhaps after stretches of calm, you may be suddenly swept out of control by forces beyond you. It's then that a flimsy air mattress doesn't provide much comfort or security!

Life for children should be secure, beautiful, and exciting, but it simply isn't always that way. There are forces that cause hurt, pain, and fear—just as there are forces that give life, love, and joy. Most of their lives are sprinkled with a variety of these influences.

This book is about children—*all* children. And it is about ministry—yours and mine, as individuals and as members of congregations. The author, Dorlis Glass, shares a vision of mutual ministry that happens when we make a move to improve the quality of children's lives, and children in turn enrich our lives.

As you read, keep real children in mind—their hopes, hurts, and struggles, their gifts, strengths, and abilities. Often we become overwhelmed by the vast need, by the unending task of improving the physical, emotional, and spiritual conditions of their lives. We know we can be in ministry with children in our relationships as parents, teachers, leaders, neighbors, pastors, friends, professional workers. And we see all children as *our* children—sons and daughters, pupils, friends, relatives, neighbors, children down the road or across town, and those we've never even met in places far away! The scope can be overpowering!

It is my hope that this book will contribute to your deepening awareness of . . .

—The life situations of children and their hopes, hurts, struggles, and aspirations;
—The responsibility for children in our congregations, families, and communities;

— The ministry that happens as individuals, groups, and congregations seek to improve the quality of children's lives;
— The urgency to choose a beginning place for ministry with children, and to *act;*
— The joy and depth of grace-filled moments that come when we take part in a mutual ministry with children.

Indeed, an intentional ministry with children may be much like riding down the rapids on an air mattress. It definitely will not be smooth sailing! *But,* along with the rough spots, the risk, fear, even danger, will also come new visions of what being faithful involves. There *is* something you can do!

Are you prepared for a ministry without boundaries?

BARBARA P. GARCÍA
Director, Development of Children's
and Marriage Growth Ministries
Section on Ministry of the Laity
General Board of Discipleship
The United Methodist Church

A Letter

Dear friend—whoever, wherever you are:

We've probably never met. Maybe we've passed in a hallway or spent a few hours in a seminar somewhere, but even then we probably don't know each other well. Yet that doesn't matter much, does it? What is important is who we are—persons who love children and are seeking ways to nurture, to enrich, and to widen the horizons of children everywhere.

Thus, in a sense, we are old friends, for we both chose to spend much of our lives holding the hands of small ones, giggling with the pre-schoolers, roughing the hair of the first graders, and challenging the minds and spirits of older children. We seek for them all the good things we have experienced and wish for them an even brighter, more peaceful tomorrow.

In this book I will be sharing with you the stories of children I have known and who have influenced my life. Promise that you will share with others the delights and the challenges of children close to you and create in them a higher level of appreciation for childhood.

I once heard a story about a little girl whose family moved to a new neighborhood. On their first Sunday, they walked together to a church near their new home. A few days later, the child wandered from her front yard and became lost. A neighbor who was working in her own yard discovered the wandering child, tears streaming down her cheeks, and called the police. On his return trip to the station with the little girl, the officer drove around several blocks hoping that the tiny one sitting beside him would recognize her home. Instead she pointed to a big building with a cross on top. "Take me there," she said. "That's the church. Take me there, and I can find my way."

I used to wonder if that story were true. There's a part of me that wants answers to questions like that. But there's also a part of my nature which allows me, even pushes me, to discover the many truths in Jesus' parables and to experience the awe of symbolism and color. So now I ask, "Does it matter whether that child truly existed or was a parable? Whether fact or fiction, isn't her affirmation the vision of what the church should be?"

So it is that we who love children look to the church as a place and a people whose ministry will nurture children and will enable them to make their way in the world, more certain of who they are as children of God and participants in the community of faith. This is a ministry that holds its own children close; yet it reaches out to all children of the community. It is *a ministry without boundaries.*

As we explore and share our dreams, let's ask ourselves this question: "What would such a ministry, one without boundaries, mean to us personally, to our congregation, to the children we touch, and to the world in which we all live, love, and serve?"

DORLIS BROWN GLASS

Catch the Vision.

Two-month-old Charles William wiggled slightly in the pastor's arms, only vaguely aware of the drops of water that touched his head and the voices that welcomed him into the church and pledged to support him. As the strains of a hymn stirred his consciousness, the tiny boy was taken by the pastor a few steps into the congregation and presented to a large man who took the baby gently, and as the hymn continued, walked with him through the congregation. At one point, he stopped to present this child of God to another child whose toothless smile welcomed this new brother in the faith. Later he stopped before an aging woman who looked with wonder at this tiny bridge to the future, a future she would not know.

"His name is Charles William," said someone softly. But everyone knew that the baby's name was Christian, and he belonged to them.

Thus Charles William began his journey, unaware of the first steps that had been taken for him by parents who love him and a congregation who responds to God's call and to the child's need for Christian nurture. This was the first sentence of the first page of his faith story.

Charles William and the other babies who are presented at the altars of churches throughout the world have begun their journeys in a world fraught with both problems and possibilities—as have the thousands of others who have not been baptized, who are not yet members of the household of God. Later their determination to build a better world and their abilities to dream of what that world can be may prod them to be the minds, hands, and hearts that God will use, even as God is using us, to create a better life for all children.

How can we help this happen? What skills can we help children develop? What dreams can we encourage them to dream that will point them to God?

We can help children anticipate possibilities and offer them opportunities to make choices. We can support them as they try new things—

1

whether or not they succeed. We can recognize the importance of dreaming, for only as one dreams can one venture into the unknown. In Genesis we read of Joseph, who had a special gift. He knew how to dream. Not limited by desert sands or by the threat of famine, he looked to God and dreamed of what might be. We can help children to dream, to hope, and to believe that with God's help the world can be a better place and that they can participate in making it better.

Such "possibility thinking" may have enabled a little boy to observe, "I guess there have always been bad guys, haven't there?"

"Yes, I guess there have been."

"I was just thinking—if the bad guys hadn't killed Jesus, things might be different now."

Wouldn't it be exciting to challenge and to lead that little boy to think of ways that he (and we) can make things different now? He heard the challenge of the gospel. He needs to hear the challenges of today's world.

I sat with my family in worship and looked around at the children gathered there. I found myself wishing for more children, for ours is a middle-aged congregation with fewer children than when our own three children were growing up. I then thought about the children who *are* there—including our three grandchildren—and hoped for them a safe and peaceful world, ample food and adequate homes, clean air and water, an education, and a faith to sustain them whatever they may encounter.

Once again I thought about how much we who love children need to be caught up in dreaming, for out of dreams come visions and planning. For most of us, the place to start dreaming will be our homes and our churches. But we can learn much about ourselves by looking outside ourselves at the ministries of others and discovering ideas and inspiration.

Some Churches with a Vision

There are congregations that serve children and the community by providing daycare for children under school age and after-school care for older children. Since nearly one-half of this year's marriages will end in divorce, we recognize that many of the children born of these marriages will live at least a part of their lives with only one parent, and daycare will be a necessary way of life. They will be joined by thousands of other children with two working parents. Quality daycare is an important service to children.

Churches provide other traditional ministries: Sunday schools, vacation church schools, day camps, resident camps, special summer programs, children's choir programs, Scout and Campfire programs, nursery schools, and special interest groups.

Being a congregation with a vision of service to children has little to do with size. It has everything to do with determination. A tiny congregation in the ranch country of New Mexico had its own vision: "We have twenty-three members, plus our children," shared a young mother and teacher. "Our minister drives out from his main charge for worship and leaves almost immediately. We wonder sometimes if the institutional church really cares about us, but I guess it does. It lets us do our own thing."

"What's your own thing?"

"Well, we wanted to have an old-fashioned vacation Bible school—like the ones some of us remembered from our childhood. We didn't have enough children in our own congregation, so we started advertising in the community. (The community covered a radius of thirty miles and more.) Anyhow, we began to plan, and by the time the Bible school week came around, we had ninety-two people involved. We figure that between us, we drove about a thousand miles that week!"

As our lab group marveled at this success story, the young teacher continued: "With so many children in the community, we realized that we didn't have enough space. So we began to work on an abandoned parsonage next door, and we are remodeling it to make two classrooms and a storage area. What's been so special is that everyone has participated. Even the children get to use paint rollers, and someone touches up what they miss. Now we've decided that as soon as we've finished this project, we'll start working to get indoor plumbing in the church!"

My friend updated the situation a year later. "The plumbing is almost completed, and we put in a telephone."

Indeed, some congregations have discovered a vision of new life.

"Will you come to our church and help us? We're going to start a Sunday school again," said a pastor recently.

The request came from a church that many years ago stood tall in an affluent neighborhood of a large city. As the years passed, the neighborhood changed. No longer were neighborhood children white and English-speaking. In time, the Sunday school ceased to be.

The congregation's request for help highlighted a renewed commitment to the Christian education of children in the neighborhood. "We don't know who will come, but we're going to be ready for them!" said an excited would-be teacher, as the group planned for community

3

outreach that would bring love and spiritual guidance to children in the community.

These are churches that have caught a vision of ministry to children, a ministry that has no boundaries. All ages are involved in the vision. They serve according to their abilities and receive the blessing of their gifts of love.

These congregations are reaching out to children and encouraging them to do what they are able to do. The operative word is *do*, not necessarily *understand* (at least in the way we usually think of understanding). As we touch the lives of children, they are experiencing God's love and learning what it means to be the Body of Christ.

With Hope and Joy

Take a moment to recall an experience of yours, a time when you climbed to a high place. Perhaps it was a hill, a bluff, a mountain. It was no easy task, and you stopped now and then to catch your breath, and to appreciate the broadening vista below.

Finally you were at the top—and great was your reward! Spread below was a view that you can still envision. New places were visible and old places were seen in a new perspective. The scene extended for miles and miles—you felt, perhaps, that you could see "forever." It was an exhilarating time for you.

A church seeking to grow in its ministry to children must catch a vision that will enable it to view with excitement, anticipation, trust, hope, and joy the broad vista of ministry before it. How can this happen? Do we wait quietly on the Spirit, hoping to discern the ministry God would have us undertake? Do we plunge into action, making our share of mistakes as we go? Do we somehow catch the vision as a child would catch chickenpox—from one another?

We probably do all of these. After all, we are committing ourselves to love children more—and when it comes to love, we each fall in love in our own special way and time. In these pages, we will share visions and stories of men and women who love God and love children. You may want to get a pad and pencil and begin to jot down ideas. And ask yourself, "How can we adapt these ideas in ways that will enrich the lives and Christian experiences of boys and girls we know and want to serve?"

In the second chapter of Acts, we find a model for making things happen. There we read about a group of frightened people whose

4

friend and teacher had gone. Struggling and without direction, they were confused and powerless. In an instant God intervened, and these people were empowered to do great things. The church was born.

Today God continues to be involved in the life of the church and in the world, speaking and challenging us to act. When and how is the Spirit speaking today? What does God require of us?

"What can't we live without?" a pastor asked a group of children on Mother's Day.

"Food," one child replied.

"You mean—like Chicken McNuggets?"

"Nooo!" they replied together. *"Just food."*

"What else?" There was a momentary silence.

"How about television? How about the Smurfs? Can we live without the Smurfs on Saturday morning?"

"Sure, Laura Ingalls did."

For the next couple of minutes, the discussion continued. With each suggestion, there was a clear *"nooo"* from the group.

Finally one child shared the secret. *"I know what we can't live without. We can't live without love."*

That child reminds us of our agenda: "The world can't live without love." The world would indeed die without love. Christians understand love to mean God's love—ever present, ever prodding, ever comforting. Our priority is to spread God's love in the world that children may feel it and know it as life itself.

For Personal Thought and Group Planning

1. What are some of the difficult situations children of your community are experiencing? List ten, and describe three of these briefly.

2. What kinds of programs and services do you envision to meet these needs? Choose at least one of the needs and imagine five approaches, five kinds of ministry.

3. Who might join with you in asking your congregation's leaders to include such ministries with children as priority concerns in planning?

4. For a more thorough approach to visioning and planning, secure the four-session workshop outline, *Leaders Make a Difference! Skills for Members of the Administrative Council, Administrative Board and*

Council on Ministries (see Resources, p. 61). Invite your congregation's leaders to take part in at least the first two sessions, "Our Community and Our Congregation," and "Clarifying a Vision for Our Community." Or use this material with persons concerned about ministries with all children.

2 See How They Grow.

Childhood is . . .

Childhood is a busy time.
Childhood is a fretful time.
Childhood is an exciting time.
Childhood is a happy time.
Childhood is a worrisome time.
Childhood is a sad time.
Childhood is . . . a very short time.

Our congregations will be best able to plan a ministry to children if we who are leaders understand the nature of childhood. Likewise we will be able to communicate the faith to children if we understand that children of different ages have their own special way of comprehending the faith story.

In recent years, John Westerhoff, James Fowler, and others have identified stages in the development of children's faith which are based largely upon their ages and their levels of experience. Understanding these stages helps parents and educators plan for the kinds of settings and experiences that are helpful and appropriate at each age. Recognizing predictable stages helps us to understand how we can nurture and challenge children. The researchers have said to us, "There is a way to share the good news with children that takes into consideration where they are on their faith journeys."

Listening to the Children

But if we are to learn about children, we would do well to go to the true experts, the children themselves. We will recognize that they can be

7

our teachers and encourage them to communicate with us. They are trying to be heard all along—to the point that their persistence has sometimes been annoying. Often we do not hear them because we do not know how to listen and interpret their "childrenese." Furthermore, what children determine is important may not fit nicely with our priorities. As a result, we too often turn them off and lose the valuable lessons they could teach.

It was the middle of July, and the children were gathered around the pastor who held in his hands a large program calendar. "What is this?" he asked.

"A calendar," was the unison response.

"What's a calendar for?"

Several children explained how they understood a calendar works.

"Look right here," said the wise adult. "This is a calendar for the month of July. This little square was yesterday, and this square is tomorrow."

"I'm going to be six on Thursday!" announced a little boy proudly.

"Oh . . . all right. Now let's look again at yesterday on the calendar." The pastor continued with a dissertation about how yesterday is gone. There's nothing we can do for God and others yesterday, for yesterday is no more. Similarly, he explained the predicament of trying to do something for God and others tomorrow when tomorrow isn't here yet.

"So . . ., he announced firmly, "We have today. Today we can do good things for God and others. And that makes today the best day of the whole week."

The same little boy shook his head in disbelief. "You've got to be kiddin'!"

This story reminds us of several things about childhood and its priorities. Who of us has not sat quietly in the pew on Sunday morning working mentally on a business problem or personal concern? Who has not had trouble concentrating on a Sunday school lesson when a member of the family or a close friend is facing a crisis? As hard as we might try, the sermon was not at the top of our priority list.

The boy was saying to us, "Listen to what is important in my life. It isn't that I don't care about God and others. Another time I'll think about them. Just don't tell me that there is anything more important in my six-year-old life this week than my birthday!"

The child was also telling us about how he understands the world. It is "real" and "concrete." A specific suggestion, "You might share your toys with your friends," would have provided him with a concrete example about how a caring child can serve, but "something for God and others" was much more general, and probably beyond the understanding of many of the children.

Ages and Stages

In the film, *What Do You Think?* Dr. David Elkind interviews children concerning the meaning of prayer. A preschool girl acts out her understanding by holding her hands tightly together in the traditional praying position. A boy only slightly older responds by reciting the familiar grace before meals. Both are concrete examples of a rather difficult concept. The thing to remember is that each is responding out of his or her experience and in a concrete way.

Recently a four-and-a-half-year-old visited her grandma. As was her custom, she got the dog pans and filled them with food. She then walked to the large patio door where she paused. Assuming that the child needed help with the door, a couple of adults started in her direction, but help was not what she wanted. She placed the pans on the floor, folded her hands, and began to recite, "God is great, God is good . . ."

Each age has its own delights and limitations that help determine what, how, and why children learn. At certain ages children are highly verbal, while at other ages they conceptualize difficult ideas and understand much but still cannot find the words to articulate concepts. Some ages listen and share; others ask questions and sometimes doubt. These are all characteristic of the developing child.

It is important that those working with children understand that children must go through all of these stages. One stage isn't better or more important than another; it is simply where a child *is* developmentally at that time of life. It's okay to see things concretely when you're five or six. It's okay to have trouble verbalizing concepts at eight. It's okay to ask questions and express doubts at eleven or twelve. Each stage is an important step on the road to a mature faith.

It is also important to recognize that children cannot skip stages. Just as it takes time for a newborn to begin walking, it takes time for the child to be able to experience and express faith. This growth is progressive, just as there is an orderly progression in his or her development of other skills. Each stage is both important and necessary on the faith journey.

For Personal Thought and Group Planning

1. Consider three or four children of various ages whom you know— say, a three-year-old, five-year-old, second grader, and fifth grader. How would you compare the way they think? The way they experience the faith community? Their understanding of Jesus? How do these individuals contrast with what you might expect as "standard" for each age level?

2. Can you trace your own development as a young Christian? How did your idea of God, for example, change from age to age?

3. In your congregation's plans for children's ministry do you take into account the vast differences from one age to another? Pinpoint any areas where your expectations may not be realistic, and consider alternative approaches.

Turn Down the Pressure.

In his book, *The Hurried Child,* Dr. David Elkind helps us to focus on the characteristics of childhood in the late twentieth century. He identifies some of the personal and cultural pressures children today are experiencing and provides clues about how persons who love children might help to alter the negative directions our culture is leading them.

Stressed and *pressured* are words which describe today's children. Stressed children are found in all kinds of homes—wealthy and poor, city and rural, church and non-church. Indeed they are often *our* children in *our* homes.

Children experience stress when they are hurried to grow up and to accept adult values and adult responsibilities. Dr. Elkind and other therapists, physicians, and educators hope to help children who are pressured in ways such as these:

- Children who are dressed and made up as miniature adults with the sexy, sometimes violent implications.
- Children who are taught to perform in beauty contests before they are old enough to start school. Again the issue of sex comes into play, for as we watch these children, we are aware that they are being taught to employ sexual poses to seduce the camera lens.
- Children who are encouraged to participate almost exclusively in organized team sports before their bodies are developed enough to accept the physical abuse they will take. They are told to follow, without questioning, adult rules for games when they might be exploring sandlot experiences which allow them to discover how and why rules are made.
- Children who are required to take care of themselves (and sometimes younger children) when they should be taken care of by responsible adults.
- Children who are growing up in single-parent homes without

two role models, and who may have to assume an adult role in providing a parent's emotional support.

- Children who are experiencing an ever-growing number of personal attacks—rape, incest, theft, and muggings.
- Children who are unable to put down roots, to make real friends, and to feel secure in a neighborhood, school, and church because parents are required to move frequently as a part of their work.
- Children who are discriminated against and who soon realize how unwanted they are as they see signs telling them that there is no place for them in many housing units.

Other sociologists have documented the hazards of high-rise living and indicated that children who live high above the streets show an increased level of stress proportional to their distance from the ground level. Such children may be unable to spend adequate time in outdoor play, and they are more likely to be subjected to abuse in elevators, hallways, and dark stairwells. At the same time, more apartments and fewer affordable single-family homes are being built, particularly in rapidly growing cities.

Growing Up Too Fast

Although stress appears to be an inevitable part of our culture, some of its causes can be controlled, especially those unintentionally created by parents. A great concern is the tendency in our society to encourage children to grow up too fast, sometimes out of a misguided pride that causes parents to believe their children are more capable than others.

"My child is ready for first grade *now*. I know she's only five, but she knows her letters and can read lots of words already. We've decided not to wait for public school. They won't make an exception in her case, so we're sending Betsy to a private school." We must wonder about Betsy if, later, she should be a slow adolescent and find herself behind her friends physically and emotionally.

"How can we get Jimmy into the high academic program in the second grade?" asked a mother at a coffee planned to meet Jimmy's first-grade teacher shortly after school began. What pressures will Jimmy feel? Will it be enough for his parents if he is a normal achiever? Will he be expected always to overachieve?

12

Parents need to look at the problems inherent in growing up too fast—including burnout, drug and alcohol abuse, and suicide—all of which are on the increase. Studies show a relationship between stress and illness, even the tendency for stressed children to fall victim to infectious disease. A new term *infant grief,* describes the feelings experienced by a very young child when separated from the mother. What additional pressures do such studies create in mothers who must work outside the home?

One day a gardener found a seed the likes of which he had never seen. "I wonder what would grow from this seed if I planted it." Full of curiosity, he took the mysterious seed to a place in the garden where the soil was rich and moist and where the sun shown on it daily. Carefully he planted the seed and waited. He wasn't anxious. He wasn't impatient. Although he knew nothing about the seed, his years of experience told him that he could trust the seed to know what was right for it. Seven days, ten days, three weeks—it wouldn't matter, for the seed would germinate in its own good time.

How this small seed responded to its own intuition and to the care of God and the gardener is a parable of growth. Newborn babies enter life with certain instincts—to breathe, to suck, to open and close their eyes. Left alone, children do these things automatically. They will grow if properly nourished. They will instinctively cling to those who provide them with nourishment. We can influence the environment—adding vitamins, sterilizing utensils, drawing the drapes—as we might influence the environment of the flower when we add light, moisture, and food. All of this special care may help to produce healthy children and brilliant blossoms, but we must recognize that to force a bloom to open before it is ready may destroy it. Dr. Elkind suggests, "He who hurries cannot walk with dignity. The child who is hurried cannot grow with dignity."

The writer of Ecclesiastes tells us that "for everything there is a season." Might he be suggesting that . . .

- It takes time for a toddler to explore the texture of carpet and the blades of green grass.
- It takes time for a kindergartner to learn about wagons and tricycles; twenty-inch two-wheelers will come later.
- It takes time to grow, to climb trees, to throw balls, to dress dolls.
- It takes time to be a parent, to supervise television, to help children learn how to make choices, to plan and prepare meals,

13

to keep them from harm. (That's an adult responsibility, isn't it—keeping children from harm.)

Other Sources of Stress

Another problem for children is that stressed children are generally being reared by stressed parents. There are the very real problems of economics—families living in poverty, parents facing the loss of family homes and farms that have given stability to their lives for generations, families with two employed parents, families headed by one parent, parents so preoccupied with their upward climb that they are unable to focus on the needs of all members of the family, parents suffering from physical and emotional burnout. What can be done? What part can the church play in finding helpful answers?

The media are both friend and enemy to children. Fine educational programs and films enrich the lives of many boys and girls, while others create new problems. There is the heavy commercialization accompanying cartoons, telling children that to be happy they must have this or that. Sex and violence are the rule on most evening television programs. A new phenomenon has appeared in television, the "superchild" who can work out problems between fighting parents or fuming friends and who, by the example he or she sets, suggests unrealistic goals for children.

For Personal Thought and Group Planning

1. How can the church be intentional about relieving the stress being experienced by children in today's society? What programs can your church initiate to eliminate or lessen these tensions—with parents in your congregation and in your community?

2. In a time when children are increasingly vulnerable to violence, what steps can your congregation take to lessen the assaults on children in your community?

Be the Church with Children.

As we begin to plan for ministries with children, we who love children need to identify for ourselves what is happening in our midst. One way to accomplish this task is to invite a group of concerned parents and leaders to participate in an awareness-building experience. Ask that they read the daily newspaper and watch a daily evening television news broadcast for a prescribed period of time, keeping a log of issues relating to or affecting children. Their lists might look something like this:

- The death from malnutrition and starvation of hundreds of thousands of children in the third world nations
- Accounts of physically and emotionally battered and sexually abused children
- Statistical data concerning teenage pregnancy, especially among early teens
- Children who receive organ transplants, and the trauma of other parents who give this gift of life even as their own children die
- The crisis in America of inadequate child care
- Children who bear the scars of frequent moves made necessary by the work patterns of their parents
- Children who live in poverty, both in the United States and in other parts of the world
- School children who participate in a food drive for famine victims in other lands
- Children who face displacement when their farm homes are sold and new homes in a new culture must be found
- Parents of disabled children suing their school district for daily nursing care
- Children and youth who are committing suicide in alarming proportions
- A friend who accidentally shoots and kills his playmate

- Children who disappear from their home, school, or playground with no indication of their whereabouts
- "Latchkey" children, who may live in fear and loneliness
- Increased numbers of children victimized by child pornography and child prostitution
- Poverty-ridden parents who sell their infants
- Children who face continuing stress and pressure from an over-organized society

Many of the problems facing the children of your community will be the same as those faced by children everywhere. Sometimes special pressures affect a particular area. When this happens, the congregation will need to discover the special concerns which it can address and seek ways to be in ministry—with food pantries, clothing banks, child care, hot lunches, or the like, while parents are putting their lives together again. Families under these kinds of stress are vulnerable to spouse and child abuse, and the church may find that it best serves children when it provides opportunities for family counseling to highly stressed families.

How can the church serve these overwhelming needs of children and their families? How can we possibly make a difference? We can, you know—by simply being the church: by caring for each other, by reflecting God's grace, by being intentional in our ministries with children.

We Care for One Another.

Sitting quietly in the pastor's study, a family weeps with pain, a pain made more unbearable because of the isolation its members feel. What concerns might members of this family need to share: a sexually abused or battered child? a child on drugs or alcohol? a pregnant teenager? a teenage son whose girlfriend is pregnant? the threat or reality of suicide? a runaway son or daughter? a crumbling marriage, financial ruin and the loss of a home, the death or terminal illness of a child?

"This has never happened to anybody we have known," cry the distraught parents. "How can we face our friends, especially the people at church?" asks the father in despair. Pastors tell us (and we who really look and listen are aware) that many families drop out of church because they are certain that their particular tragedy has never been

16

experienced by others, and that nobody will understand. It is sad when they leave, but it is doubly tragic that when they leave, they are alone!

What if . . . the church were to sponsor a group where parents could share their concerns in an atmosphere of trust and love even before a crisis happens?

What if . . . parents could share their values and listen to the views of other parents? At times all parents have known the vicarious peer pressure in a daughter's plea, "But, Mom, Becky's mother says it's okay." Or, "Dad, none of the other kids have to be in by that time." Or, "Hey, everybody in the fifth grade is wearing eye make-up." Sharing groups can help parents reach mutual agreements and formulate family guidelines reflecting a consensus of the community. Although each family would ultimately develop its own guidelines, it would do so recognizing the values of the other members of the parenting community.

What if . . . the pastor were to participate in the parent group and help to create a community so strong and loving that when an emergency arises in the group, a cadre of supportive adults were ready to sit with the family of a runaway or critically ill child?

We Reflect God's Grace.

When I talk with children about the meaning of baptism, I sometimes explain that it is a symbol of God's reaching out and saying to us, "I love you." A part of what makes that kind of love so special is that I don't have to ask God to love me. God loves me because God is a loving God.

When we apply this understanding of God's freely given, unconditional love to their relationships with the community's children and their parents, especially those experiencing problems, we say to them, "You're okay. You may make mistakes, but they don't make you a bad person. You can be forgiven—you *are* forgiven. You can start again. We love you as God loves you, and we will support you as you begin again."

Children who are so embraced will understand that they are valuable, lovable, important. Hopefully they will not need a gang to support them, because *we* will support them. They will not harm themselves by overdosing on drugs or driving under the influence of alcohol in a desperate attempt to be accepted. *We* accept them. That is what God has taught us to do.

We Plan for Ministry.

The sixth chapter of Acts tells how the early Christian church struggled to be in mission and in ministry to the world and to its own membership. The Hebrew community had brought from its Jewish tradition a structure that provided care for those with special needs. Unlike their former Jewish brothers and sisters, Greek Christians lacked a structure and soon became aware that the needy among them were not receiving the support of the group. Peter devised a plan, selecting seven deacons who would care for those in need.

Like the New Testament church, today's congregation delegates persons and groups to be responsible for special ministries: education, worship, stewardship, missions, and other areas of work. One area for which clearly designated leadership is essential is the congregation's ministry with children—children within the church, in the community, in the world. Such a leader may be called a coordinator of children's ministry.

By whatever name, it is the responsibility of this leader to help leaders in all the work areas of the congregation see the needs of children and find ways of ministering with them, and ways the children themselves can contribute to the ministry of the church. As an advocate for children, the coordinator raises questions about the ways children are being included in the life of the community and congregation.

Because it is the responsibility of this leader to share concerns and to make suggestions to all program groups, he or she is not limited by the boundaries of a particular work area. The coordinator's role is to be a servant of all children in *a ministry without boundaries.*

The arena for ministries may be the church building itself. It may also be the home, the school, the playground, or a nearby civic club. It may be beyond the immediate neighborhood—an inner housing project, a children's hospital, a public school seeking assistance in tutoring. Or the arena may be still further away—children who are hungry and ill in many places in our nation and in the world. Or . . .

We are all called to this unlimited ministry with God's children. Whether or not the congregation has a person designated to lead in children's ministries, this work is ours to do—in at least two senses:

- Individually, we each have a ministry with children. As parents, neighbors, friends, aunts and uncles, grandparents, in our jobs and in our leisure, we have countless opportunities to care about children. In acts as simple as a smile in the grocery store or as

18

demanding as advocacy before the city council, we can be their friends.

- Within our congregations, as members and leaders, we can take part in ministries with children. In each planning and administrative body of the church, we can represent the children of the community and speak up for their needs. If needed, we can take their side in issues related to policy, program, staff, and finance. We can volunteer as leaders and workers in various programs. We can simply "be there" when children are involved, lending our support to children, parents, and leaders.

What does it mean to "be the church" with children—to care for them, to reflect God's grace for them, to get into ministry with them? This is a question with no simple, ready-made answers. But it is a question each disciple of Jesus Christ, and each congregation of his followers must ask . . . and answer.

For Personal Thought and Group Planning

1. Develop your own statement of what it means to "be the church" with children. If your congregation has a "statement of mission," apply it to the children of your community and church.

2. How can your congregation support all its members in their individual ministry with children of the community? List ten things.

3. With what community agencies might you encourage persons to work as part of their ministry with children?

4. What special issues in children's ministry face your leaders, issues that may need the support of church members, church leaders of the area, or specialists from the community? How can this support be enlisted?

Include Them in Worship.

One persistent issue in children's ministry has to do with their participation in congregational worship. Questions may sound like this: "How old should children be when they begin to attend worship services? How much do children understand? Are they learning enough to justify the distractions they cause? Is it worth the stress their presence causes their parents?"

There are congregations that have determined that junior church or child care is the answer for them. But many more celebrate the presence of children in their congregation, and realize the vital importance of children learning to worship and sharing in that core happening in the lives of Christians! "The older members of the congregation are my children's foster grandparents," said a young mother. "It's tough living so far away from family. But when Norma puts her arms around Sammy, he understands what it is like to have an older person love him."

An older woman nearby joined in: "The children are the grandchildren I can't hug because mine are too far away. It's worth the sound of dropped pencils just to be able to see them there and to touch them once in a while. I only wish my grandchildren were sitting beside them."

But do they understand anything that is happening?
How much are they participating?
Are they really worshiping?

The second grader's fingers stayed busy during most of the worship service, creating first cars and then robots from the two Go-Bots he had stowed in his pockets. He paused long enough to sing the first verse of a familiar hymn and to recite the Lord's Prayer with the congregation. Nobody challenged his toys, for he was quiet and bothered no one.

Late in the service, the pastor received the confirmation class and gave each confirmand an olive-wood cross.

"One of our church families brought you these crosses from the Holy

Land," the pastor explained. Instantly the child's eyes darted to his grandfather. "Was that you?"

As the granddad nodded a response, he wondered, "How much has the little boy really heard while he was manipulating his toys? What has he learned? What growth has taken place that nobody had reason to suspect?"

Helping Children Take Part

There are those who have said, "Our children are the church of tomorrow." More and more, congregations are embracing their children and adding, ". . . and they are a part of the church today." This insight leads them to join with those who suggest that "the journey itself is the destination." There is a value in childhood that should be appreciated, both as an end in itself and as a stepping stone to the future.

Many pastors and worship leaders look to children as fellow worship leaders. Children sing in choirs, sing solos, and serve as acolytes. They are liturgists and dancers, instrument players and banner bearers. They are visible. They participate and serve. They worship alongside adults and youth. Occasionally they are invited to serve as ushers and servers of the elements in Holy Communion. But whether as leader or participant, it is important that children be part of the community of faith at worship.

Many churches provide child care for preschool children. In these settings, the children experience activities ranging from babysitting to an extended educational time. Some congregations use this time to prepare five-year-old children for worship by helping them become familiar with the worship service as they examine the bulletin and learn common prayers and hymns, the Doxology, and the Gloria Patri. When children reach first grade and are encouraged to attend worship with their parents, they do so with some understanding of what will happen there.

There are congregations that provide special worship guides or activity packets for children to use during the service to focus their attention on the worship experience. Many are designed to help children become involved in and aware of what is happening in the service. An increasing number of congregations provide opportunities for parents and children to learn about the sacraments by participating, either together or by age levels, in special classes. Parent education sessions have proved especially valuable in communities where families move frequently and where a congregation's membership does not suggest a long United Methodist tradition.

"Daddy," said a little girl as the family drove to church. "Is this the day we go up and sit on our knees and drink red Kool-Aid?"

"No, this isn't the week we have Communion," her startled father responded.

"I like it when Dr. Slack says, 'When you eat this, remember that God loves you.'"

Years have passed. That little girl now has children of her own, children who accompany their parents to the Communion table and are told again and again how much God loves them. This is our understanding of Holy Communion put into words that young children can understand and feel.

A Special "Children's Time"?

The children's sermon, sometimes called the children's time, is a popular addition to the worship service in many areas. Those who advocate these special moments directed to the children of the congregation say that it is a time when children can be close to the minister in a personal way. It is a time when children are encouraged to move about, for they do need to stretch those muscles. It is a time when they receive a message planned just for them.

A pastor who serves two churches and who must use the Sunday school hour for traveling between them speaks of the children's time this way: "It is the only time that I can be with the children of my smaller congregation on a regular basis. My home is near the other church so I'm at the smaller one only a few hours a week. I wouldn't give up my children's time for anything. It's the most special thing I do."

There are many who choose not to include a children's time in the service. They point out that it disrupts the order of worship, that it often becomes a time when children are manipulated and used as a diversion to entertain the congregation, and that those presenting the "message" often do not understand the development of children, and present messages beyond their comprehension. Many of these churches prefer to involve children throughout worship in other ways: by singing a hymn they have learned in Sunday school, by including a prayer written by a children's class, by using banners made by classes, by including a song

23

by the children's choir, and by using references in the sermon to which children can relate.

It is vital that the pastor become involved in the lives of children in important and meaningful ways. The minister of a large-membership church was eager to participate in the Christian education program of the congregation. One of the problems he faced was that the worship services and Sunday school classes were held simultaneously. Because he was committed to a ministry with children, he explained to his congregation that on some occasions he would be late arriving in the pulpit. Others started the service and led the opening liturgy while he visited the children's classes when invited. Knowing the approximate time schedule, he arranged to arrive in the pulpit during the hymn which preceded the sermon. "I've been visiting the children," he would announce with a smile. Hopefully, by his testimony to the importance of relationship with the children, in time they can have opportunity to attend worship and Sunday school at different hours.

The Sacraments

With the sacraments more at the center of United Methodist worship, we are discovering exciting ways to include children in this special time. One pastor invites the children of the congregation to the altar, where they stand with the parents and family members of an infant during the baptism. At the completion of the ritual, he introduces the baby to the children as their new brother or sister in the faith.

In another church, children make greeting cards in Sunday school for the baby that is to be baptized. The cards are presented to the parents by a representative child following the baptism. Still another congregation takes a few minutes in the service to write "I wish for you . . ." cards to the baby.

"Why is it important for children to be a part of the community of faith gathered for worship?" There are many answers to this often-heard question—children's involvement, their participation with their families, their exposure to great music, to scripture reading, to prayer, to church leaders—what else? As you consider the answer you might give, let me share mine:

Our world offers children too little opportunity to sense the security of permanence. The church as a worshiping community is one place where children can feel connected. As they participate in this special hour, they sense and perhaps say, "I am a part of something that has been important for hundreds of thousands of years. And I believe that it is something that will continue to be, for God is there."

There is another value as well: We are richer because of the participation of children in worship. They bring their particular gifts to this intergenerational time of celebration. They help to remind us that we are God's household, a people of diverse abilities and understandings. In their vulnerability they remind us that it is not our own strength but God's gracious love that supports us all. In their need they call us to ministry, not only to them but to "the least of these" wherever and however they are hurting.

For Personal Thought and Group Planning

1. What is your congregation's policy regarding the presence in the worship service of children of various ages? What are the strengths and weaknesses of this policy? In what group could you explore this further?

2. How are children now helped to take a meaningful part in your congregation's worship? By parents? By the pastor? By the order of worship? Through music? How could their participation be enriched?

3. Secure and study the *Children and Worship Resources Packet* (Discipleship Resources) which includes the following leaflets: *Keep Them in Their Place?; Worship Readiness: Preparing Children for Congregational Worship; Worship Guides for Children: Adapting the Sunday Bulletin,* and *Preparing Parents and the Congregation for the Baptism of Infants and Children.* Develop recommendations and work with the pastor, other worship leaders, and parents in refining them.

4. How do your children take part in the sacraments, baptism and Holy Communion? If you are not already using it, secure copies of the *Communion Book for Children* (Discipleship Resources), a colorful, follow-along guide to the service.

Count on Their Stewardship.

I was a bit late getting to the "coffee-house" sing-along at a recent children's conference. The only space left was on the floor between the platform and the first row of chairs. I had been sitting there sipping a cold drink for several moments when two little girls wandered into the area and looked about for space to sit down. The older child found a spot; the little one, a child of four or five clutching her doll, continued her search. To my surprise, the space she chose was my lap—and she, too, staked her claim.

"Who is she?" asked my friend.

"I have no idea."

"I guess she needed a grandmother."

"Maybe she needed lap time," I responded.

There she sat, swaying with the music, clapping after every song. Finally she stood up, smiled at me, and left. I watched as she found her way back five rows to her very pregnant mother. "It *was* lap time she needed," I laughed.

Since that evening I have wondered if she somehow recognized in me a grandmother who missed her own little ones and who needed at that very moment the nurture of a little girl willing to share her softness and her doll. There's a radical concept—mutual ministry between a child and a grandmother! But every grandparent knows it happens.

Yes, children—all children—have gifts to give. We can count on them as joyful givers. We can count on their stewardship.

A Gift of Kindness

From boxes under the bed, sacks tucked in closets, and an overflowing car trunk came treasures which would soon become dozens of valentines for a retirement home. The creators of such beauty were second and third graders in an after-school program at a church in Iowa.

When their gifts were completed, the children went to the home to sing "valentine carols," songs about love. Waiting for them at the door was an elderly man who made it his job to greet all visitors to the home. Reflecting on her experiences, the teacher who shared this story said that in her many visits she has never seen him with a visitor of his own. She tells her story this way:

"Jeff's valentines were almost gone. There was only one left in his hand."

"Is it all right if I give it to that man?" he asked, pointing to the little man who had greeted him.

"You may give it to anyone you wish."

Jeff walked to where the man stood alone and held out the valentine. "I didn't know you would have one for me," the old man said with tears streaming down his cheeks.

Outside the little boy asked, "Why did he cry?"

"How do you explain the stewardship of kindness, hope, and loving human relationships?" the teacher asked us.

Gifts of Special Children

More and more, our church is learning to celebrate the value of children with handicapping conditions, some of whom will never see the tomorrows about which most of us dream. We are coming to understand that time spent with a child whose body and/or mind cannot fully develop is valuable time. These are God's children, and they remind us that God loves each one of us. Churches throughout the nation have organized Sunday school classes for children with special needs. They have also followed the example of public education by placing these children in classes with other children their own age. Learning together can provide an opportunity for sharing the gifts and love of each child in an affirming and nurturing way.

Duke was short in stature, but Robert thought he was a giant as he looked up at the man who strolled beside him toward their special place out under a tree in the churchyard. Robert had been born with a serious hearing impairment that made it impossible for him to participate in a regular classroom. Duke had two young-adult children, one of them mentally retarded. It was his understanding and care for special-needs children that prompted Duke to respond to a plea for someone who would go with Robert into the third-grade classroom, sit across from him, and serve as his interpreter. The boy could lip-read, and with Duke's help, he "heard" many of the stories. Duke was generous with his time and his gift of love.

Other ministries for special children are emerging. One area sponsors a resident camp for disabled children which is called SEEK (Summer Events for Exceptional Kampers). Because of the special needs of these campers, the ratio of adult and youth counselors to children is three to five. Every child is visited by a counselor before camp in order to gather information and design the most appropriate camp experience. Medical personnel are on the grounds.

A remarkable story has emerged from SEEK, that of a young man who came first as a child camper and is now serving as a junior counselor. He has spina bifida but he is a determined young man, one with limitations, who has learned to serve and share—acknowledging his special giftedness. One can only imagine what his example says to the young campers as they seek to find their own gifts for sharing.

Several years ago, a large Kansas church began to provide Sunday morning educational experiences for dozens of children and youth with handicapping conditions. It is their church home, a place where they know they are accepted and loved. Their parents know it too. The class is led by people who have been challenged by an opportunity for a different kind of ministry. Together, leaders and young people are growing in the knowledge of who they are and *whose* they are—stewards, care-takers of the many and varied gifts of a loving Creator.

Interpreting Stewardship to Children

How do we teach children to share? What do we mean when we say that they can be stewards? Are we suggesting that they lend a toy, a T-shirt, or a tape—and take it back later? That may be exactly what we mean with very young children. But are there *values* we can teach them to share—such as love, gentleness, a caring smile, an act of kindness, a prayer for hope and peace, the gospel acted out?

Is not stewardship a matter of helping them to learn to live in anticipation of God's future for Planet Earth, the coming day of shalom? This dream of a better tomorrow requires a foundation of faith—and daily discipline marked by determination, perseverance, and optimism.

A sixth-grade girl described the events of an icy day: "We tried to climb the hill. We'd take a step or two holding on to each other, or anything along the way that would help us climb. Then we'd start to slide back. Sometimes we'd slide all the way back, but usually it would be just a little bit. Then we'd try again."

The picture became clear. Forward two steps, back one-and-a-half—forward one, back one—forward three, back two. . . .

"Oh my," said an adult who was listening to the child tell her story. "It hardly seems worth the effort. You made such little progress considering the effort you made."

"I don't feel that way at all," said her friend. "I'd settle for all that slipping anytime if I thought that at the end of the final climb, I would find a new friend, clean air—or peace!"

Helping children to discover who they can be as stewards requires that we help them to develop patience and perseverance, that we encourage them to set priorities and goals toward which they can work. It requires that *we* live in response to each moment, each task, each call to discipleship. Our lives, our awareness, attitudes, affirmations, and actions can lead them to be faithful stewards of God's world.

A Response to God's Grace

Where did it all begin, this idea of stewardship? The children can tell us, for they're singing the answer. "We love because God first loved us." The First Letter of John tells us that it was God who modeled love, and humans responded. Parents and teachers model how to share and how to care, and children respond. The church models self-giving, and young persons make a similar response.

There is a very special congregation that believes and demonstrates this modeling concept with remarkable and rewarding consequences. Each year the eighth graders are treated by the church to a week of backpacking. There is no charge to the children; it is a gift from the congregation. Nothing is required, but something is expected—a miracle!

A covenant or promise is made between the church and the young

*teens almost without words, for they begin almost immediately to ask,
"What can we do to show love to those who have loved us?"*

*A year, indeed years, of service begins—service such as child care,
help with church dinners, and light yardwork. The covenant is not a
bribe; it is response which includes caring, sharing, loving, and doing. It
is an investment in tomorrow that the congregation makes each year,
and as they participate, the young people learn that stewardship is joy,
fellowship, and love. They love, their congregation loves—because God
first loved.*

As we seek ways to lead children in becoming faithful stewards, we
can help them learn that giving is a natural response to God's love. We
will encourage them to care for their bodies and for all that is around
them. We will show them how by participating with them in picking up
soft-drink cans in the parking lot or planting flowers in the spring. We
will give willingly, cheerfully, and generously of our time, our abilities,
and our finances.

Should we expect children to be good stewards? The answer is yes.
To deny children the right to give is to deny them a chance to be
partners with God and their fellow human beings. Whether they are
sharing labor, money, or a concern for others, children, just as adults,
should be challenged to leave the world a little bit better than when they
entered it.

For Personal Thought and Group Discussion

1. What gifts have you observed children sharing with others—not
just physical things, of course, but words, actions, and attitudes as well?
What gift have you received from a child lately? What can we do to
support and channel such giving?

2. What ministries is your church offering children with handicapping
conditions? How are their distinctive gifts being offered and received?
Secure and study the book, *We Don't Have Any Here* (Discipleship
Resources), a guide to planning ministries with disabled persons. With
others, consider what new ministries might be developed for such
children in your community.

3. How is faithful stewardship nurtured in the families of your church?
How does the church school help? What new visions of stewardship do
you have for the children of your congregation? Your community?

Secure copies of the six-session, children's study of stewardship, *I've Got Something to Share (Leader's Guide* and *Student Leaflets),* and plan for use with third through sixth graders (available from Discipleship Resources).

7 Join with Their Parents.

In a television interview, the late Henry Fonda recalled a special day. Mr. Fonda explained that although his father had not altogether approved of his decision to become an actor, the older man had attended various productions in which his son had a part.

One evening the family gathered to see a new play. Later each one offered his or her critique of Henry's performance. "Perhaps you might have . . ." "Maybe it would have been better if . . ." "I was thinking that you should have . . ." Quietly the older man lowered the paper behind which he had positioned himself and said simply and emphatically, "He was perfect!"

Self-image and *self-esteem* are terms often used by persons who love children. We recognize that feeling good about themselves is vital if boys and girls are to be emotionally healthy. This isn't a new idea. Thousands of years ago, the inspired writers of scripture shared this insight, but it has lain undiscovered by many of us.

"You shall love the Lord your God with all your heart and soul and might, and your neighbor as yourself." For a long time, many of us understood that this verse was telling us only how we should relate to God and others. But then we began to understand that it directs us to love ourselves as well.

"You mean, it's all right if I love myself?" we asked. "Isn't that conceit?"

With the help of theologians and psychologists we came to understand that we can only respect and love others if first we respect and, yes, love ourselves! There is, then, an important scriptural basis for helping all human beings to possess a positive self-image, and it points us in the direction of living in love with the Creator and all creation.

Children need to like themselves, to feel that they are important and worthy. Experts tell us that children with low self-images are more likely to become victims of drugs, alcohol, sexual violence, and other violations of the spirit and the body. Peer pressure is felt more strongly by those who do not recognize that they are worthwhile and have the right to help determine what will happen to them.

United Way agencies, the Red Cross, and civic groups have been organized to provide assistance to persons with special problems. The church, because of its long history of trust in the community, is able to provide special support too. Parents are frequently willing to trust the church to love and tend their children, even in traumatic times.

New Needs for Sex Education

Sexual activity is a normal, God-given, human function and a proper way to express love. Still, sexuality is an area of human relationships which has caused problems in every generation. In our time teenage pregnancies are increasing and younger teens are increasingly involved in these pregnancies. Venereal diseases are common even among children, both because of sexual contact and because children have not received guidance in such basic concerns. Children in alarming numbers are being victimized by prostitution and pornographic rings. Sexual abuse, sometimes perpetrated by family members, appears also to be increasing. Incest is so commonly reported that it is no longer a word found primarily in an Old Testament list of sins.

Recently some parents who must leave their children in child-care facilities became aware that their children were being victimized by persons whom they had believed to be trustworthy. Schools and churches have sought assistance from persons who are trained to help children learn what to do in case they are threatened or violated.

The sexual abuse of children is probably not a new phenomenon. Experts suggest that children may always have been prey to individuals who, through psychological coercion or greater physical strength, have abused children. Most authorities agree that too little sex education is available to children, and at least one family-court judge has suggested that sexual abuse of children will not be stopped until children are given the psychological and language tools to be able to explain what is happening to them.

Certain, often unavoidable, aspects of today's culture place children in jeopardy. Although this section will focus on sexual violence against children, it should be recognized that all forms of violence are at issue. With the realization that children are being battered, raped, and emotionally abused, persons who love children may be called to cope with some or all of the following issues:

34

1. More children are being cared for by babysitters and in child-care agencies than ever before. Economic conditions require two family incomes, increasing numbers of women pursue careers, and an increasing number of single-parent households require daycare. Thus daycare centers and in-home caregivers are replacing the parental care of former generations.

2. Many children live in homes with adults who are not their birth parents or relatives. Stepparents, stepbrothers and sisters, and other non-related teenagers and adults are living in close proximity with children, providing opportunities for intimacies not formerly readily available.

3. Thousands of "latchkey" children spend two or more hours daily alone without supervision and protection. They are especially vulnerable to abusive strangers, neighbors, and family members.

4. Parents are discovering and reporting sexual abuse in increasing numbers, and the media are reporting the exploitation of children, thus heightening our awareness of it.

Church and Parents in Partnership

Many churches are cooperating with trained mental health personnel whose programs and educational techniques are designed to protect children by giving them the vocabulary and the persistence to call for help, to let them know that children are always right to ask for assistance. When child-care facilities are offered by a church, those responsible will take great care in the persons they hire and will provide for supervision of both the children and the caregivers.

A few years ago, it was assumed that sex education was almost exclusively the responsibility of the home and family. Whatever formal sexuality training a child received was dependent upon his or her family and, to a lesser extent, on health classes at school. Many children received no sexuality education and were dependent upon friends and street talk for information about their own bodies. For many children this education came too late.

Recently the church has become a partner with parents in this important ministry. Denominations are providing resources for parents and/or small group leaders to use with children in the home or in special settings. A new resource for mentally retarded youth and young adults, produced by the National Council of Churches, includes a five-session sexuality series.

A United Methodist program—including the resource for older elementary children, *God Made Us: About Sex and Growing Up*—encourages parents to participate in a four- to six-hour seminar before their children take part in their own class. The program provides for a generous adult-child ratio, careful monitoring of classroom experiences, and a time for questions and discussion. In adapting the resource for their own groups, many leaders include parents at different times throughout the workshop and close with a time of intergenerational sharing and worship. Perhaps the greatest value in the program is that boys and girls come to understand that it is all right to wonder, to make believe, and to ask questions of persons who care about them—their parents, teachers, and other adult confidants.

It may be that the church can best love children by offering parents the opportunity to share concerns and questions. Consider the special needs of families today. With the increasing number of single-parent families, many children are growing up without both male and female role models. Single parents need opportunities to talk with each other: "This is what I am feeling and fearing, . . ." shares a mother, and in so doing she may enable the single father to talk with his children about some feelings and concerns inherent in being female. Likewise, a single mother can gain needed insights and vocabulary while listening to the questions of a concerned father.

Other concerns arise in such meetings:

- Some adults received little or no formal sexuality education as children or youth, and are misinformed. Here they may voice questions and clarify what they have come to understand as truth.
- Values of parents are discussed and problems voiced. In this climate of mutual concern, parents may discover that other parent sessions would be helpful, some pertaining to issues beyond that of sexuality.
- Parents will have the opportunity to discuss how much home and family relationships affect their children's understanding of their own sexuality. Sexuality training begins in the early years when children are hugged, touched, and caressed as infants by those who love them. As they observe a gentle, affectionate relationship between parents, young children receive their first sense of the loving way people can relate to one another. This is not to suggest that young children are to witness sexual inter-

36

course, which would very likely confuse or frighten them; it does suggest that they should witness tenderness.

Being a Whole Person

The church is helping to redefine sex education. When one's sexuality is understood as being a whole, loving person, concerned about self and others, it is taken out of the back alleys and permitted to live in the healthy light of day. The human body becomes appreciated as a good gift from God, another of all the good gifts that have been given us, and it is worthy of our care.

Once again parents and leaders are asked to recognize the important issue of self-esteem as a balance to peer pressure. As in the issues mentioned earlier, children relate in more loving ways when they can say, in effect, "I like myself. I can make good judgments. I want to exercise my right to make important decisions about my body."

One area has developed a learning design for older elementary children to explore drug and alcohol use and abuse, a design based on some of the same principles described above for sexuality education. The program is based on similar assumptions: Children need correct information upon which to make choices, and children who like themselves are more likely to be in control of themselves. It is easier for a child to say, "I'll make those choices for myself, thank you," when confident about his or her self-worth. The program also assumes a high level of participation by parents, who are challenged to show concern for their children by providing healthy examples for them.

For Personal Thought and Group Planning

1. In what specific ways are children's leaders of your congregation working in partnership with parents—parents both of your own children and of children in the community? Do you see needs of children that can best be met by the church and parents working together? In what areas do parents most need and want the support of the church?

2. How are children of your church and community now receiving information and values related to their sexuality? From home? School? Church? Peers? Not at all? Do you think the church has a distinctive role here? If so, what? Secure and study copies of the six-session elective

unit for elementary children, *God Made Us: About Sex and Growing Up (Student Book* and *Leader's Guide),* and plan for ways to use it.

3. Values and behavior in the area of sexuality are closely tied to personal self-esteem. List ways children come to value and like themselves. What evidence of low self-esteem do you see among children of your congregation, your community? How could you work with parents in this difficult area?

$\bigl(\!\bigr)$ Introduce Them to the World.

The kingdom is coming! The promised day of shalom is on its way! The God of Moses, the God of Jesus, is going before us, drawing us into this planet's future, a future of wholeness, peace, and justice. That is the vision and promise of the Bible. Do you believe in it?

This shalom vision is our call to mission in the world, for it is only through the partnership of God and God's people, laboring toward the vision, that the promise can come true. Inspired by this hope, we feed the hungry, care for the sick, clothe the naked. We challenge the tired old ways of war and the greedy powers that oppress "the least of these." We proclaim the good news of God's love for all and seek to embody this love in our personal action, our institutions, our public policies. We do not always succeed—but we are obedient to the vision.

Because we are the people of hope, we are in mission. And because we love children, we support *their* hope and guide *their* mission. We introduce them to the world, to its ugliness as well as to its beauty. And we find ways to help them respond with their gifts, to take an active part in ministry, and thus to work for and welcome the coming kingdom of God.

"What are you wearing on your arm, John?"

"It's a prayer bracelet. The teenagers in our church are on a work trip. They're in Appalachia putting new roofs on homes and building rooms on others. It's an all-church project. Those of us who couldn't go are supporting their work with money for supplies and with our prayers. We're wearing these hospital bracelets with the name of one of our kids on it. We pray for them and their work daily."

"Look, my bracelet has Barbara Phillip's name on it," said six-year-old Kelly. *"I pray for her every night."*

Resources are available: mission studies in denominational curriculum and from Friendship Press, visits from those who have worked in the mission field, films and other media resources that tell the story, interpretive materials from agencies such as CROP, UNICEF, The Heifer Project, The United Methodist Children's Fund for Christian Mission, and field trips to agencies serving those in need. All of these focus on helping children discover ways people can help people, ways they can be part of the church's mission.

It is our responsibility as adults to make these experiences available for use in creative ways and to encourage children, once they are informed, to participate in sharing projects and experiences. By encouraging boys and girls to play games, to write and sing songs, hymns, prayers, litanies, and choral readings, leaders provide them with a language about caring. Christian responsibility may be understood, then, as something that believers do because they have hopes for loving relationships, and for a world of peace and justice.

World-mindedness requires openmindedness and the realization that people are hungry and abused for a variety of reasons: flood or drought, poor farming habits, political and economic oppression, war, lack of new breeding stock, and a multitude of concerns. Sometimes we encounter resistance in our own congregation, folks who question if people in developing countries are helping themselves, people who want to know if the starving are really grateful for all that they are receiving, and people whose bias reflects their own political and economic well-being. Children hear these issues being discussed in the home and on television and ask questions. What will we tell them?

Read again Jesus' familiar parable of the good Samaritan (Luke 10:30-37), reflecting on three questions:

- Did the Samaritan suggest to the injured man that he should get up and take care of himself?
- Did the Samaritan ask for gratitude as a condition for his gift of mercy?
- Did the Samaritan check to see if the injured man was of his religion and social class?

There are other values, things like tenacity, which must be developed if children are to become world-minded. How can we teach children that Christians never stop trying to make things better? How can we help them recognize that there will always be persons with needs, yet not discourage them with a sense of uselessness?

Helping Children Help

We have going for us a special characteristic of children: They generally want to help. Often we have heard a child say, "Let me help!" followed at once by an offer to share. Children seem to have an intuitive desire to participate in a caring community.

Yet there are other influences that help determine what children will be. Ours is a computerized world of exactness, facts, and figures, and children may forget or never really learn how to dream. At risk is their ability to understand that there is *truth* behind all of those facts. Not only is there the reality of pain—hunger, disease, famine, poverty, and war—there are also reasons they exist, and solutions, if time and resources can be made available. First, there must be a dream of a better day.

At home, at school, at church, we have opportunities to encourage children to dream and to react creatively. With their words and relationships, those who love children can offer boys and girls the opportunity to use their imaginations, to dream, and to take risks. They can allow them to realize both success and failure in a setting that does not raise fear of criticism as a block to self-discovery.

For example, we can show our children a discarded item and ask, "What can you do with it? What beautiful or useful thing can you create? It isn't really junk, you know, because you and I together can make something special of it." As we help children dream, we will talk with them about the value of all things and all people. Value doesn't come from skin color, sex, age, or religion.

It is important that people who love children listen to what they say and understand how they feel. We will hear their personal stories and invite them to share their histories. We will encourage them to listen as others share their stories and help them recognize that all of us are a part of a great history devoted, in part, to making life better for each generation. Encouraging children to test their ideas and their dreams allows them the opportunity to learn how to dream impossible dreams, a quality badly needed in this less than perfect world.

Children should have the opportunity to be with adults who have dreams, who have caught the shalom vision. How quickly children can be discouraged if their adult models bring an air of discouragement to what they do! Children are blessed if they associate with adults who talk about a happier tomorrow, peace, gentleness, kindness, love, and justice. They are even more blessed when those important adults show them by example what these words mean.

41

One July evening in 1984, I met our newest grandchild, a tiny little blond baby girl who would soon be named Lindsey Gray Glass. "Interesting name," you may ask. "Gray?"

Leon and Mary Gray were Junior High MYF counselors when our son was that age. Leon was a Dallas policeman and Mary a gentle mother and secretary.

Five years later a telephone call advised us that Leon was dead— killed in an auto accident as he returned from work. A drunk driver had backed out into traffic sending Leon's small car into a concrete bridge support. Two years later Mary died of cancer. We wept with our son, and wondered why.

Now when I hold Lindsey Gray, I remember and celebrate with her daddy the love shown and lessons taught by this special couple. We remember together that those who dream, those who share their dreams, those who serve, do make a difference.

For Personal Thought and Group Discussion

1. What are your own visions of God's future for Planet Earth? Describe your dreams. Where do these dreams come from—from what persons and experiences? In what ways did your childhood relationships and experiences contribute to your present vision?

2. For further study of the shalom vision, involve parents and teachers in a peacemaking workshop. Then develop implications for your congregation's ministry with all children.

3. How does your congregation help children get in touch with the world, its needs and its future? How do children take part in the mission of your congregation? How do they learn about the whole church's mission around the world?

4. What changes in mission education and mission participation would you recommend for your church's ministry with children?

5. How could you help children in your community "be with adults who have dreams, who have caught the shalom vision"?

Enlist Them as Peacemakers.

Rest in peace, for the mistake will not be repeated.

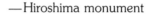

—Hiroshima monument

When asked to describe their fears, many children say that they are afraid of nuclear war. They haven't seen war, but they have seen pictures of the bombing of Hiroshima at the close of World War II, and they sense the terrible destructive force. I have not visited Hiroshima, the site of the monument which carries this pledge of peace (above). But I have visited the Holocaust Monument and Museum in Jerusalem, another place that reminds us of those grim days, and I believe that peace must be the highest priority of all for Christians. The museum contains thousands of pictures of children—children about to die and children already dead. Thousands of children died at Hiroshima also.

Today children are dying in dozens of wars around the world. Terrorism is as common for many children as a soccer game is for American children. As we think about and plan for ministry to children beyond the boundaries of our own congregations, we must include in our plans and in our prayers these children of war. We must address the issue of helping to change conditions which lead to war and terrorism.

I grew up at a time when war was real. I remember an unspoken fear when sirens pierced the night and the curtains were quickly drawn. I remember that my father would leave the house and go to the school which had been designated as a command post for the aid-raid wardens. Mother's responsibility was to check conditions on the block. My older sister, younger brother, and I remained at home alone. The enemy did not come, but we were prepared—just in case.

I remember that several years later, as a teacher, I had to herd twenty-nine first graders into a "duck and cover" position, bottoms to the classroom windows, bodies under the desks. "Heads down, boys and girls. Put your hands behind your neck and protect your head and face." Then when the bells rang, I continued, "Now we must all go outside very quickly." The assumption was that after any bombing there would be fires.

A few years later my own children began to bring home cards for us to indicate what their father and I wanted them to do in case of enemy attack. Should they come home? Stay at school? Meet us at some predetermined place? What was our choice should our worst fears become a reality? My now-grown daughter remembers her fear at the sight of those cards and those awful choices.

I remember the fallout shelters which dotted the backyards of many American homes and the terrible question that people were asking themselves, "Who will we allow inside the shelter in addition to our own family? After all, we have only so much food and water stored there."

We lived near the Texas gulf coast and experienced the panic of the Cuban missile scare. Everyone raced to the hardware store to purchase large garbage cans to store water and on to the supermarkets crowded with customers pushing carts and buying canned goods. Everyone was preparing for war. There were babies in those shopping carts and children hurrying along beside their frightened parents.

Isn't it time for the church to ask, "Who is preparing the children for peace? Who is teaching them that there are other ways to deal with anger and frustration than striking out in violence?" Isn't it time for the church to address the issue of peace?

The automobile held three passengers—a grandmother and her two grandchildren, ages eight and eleven. Christmas was approaching and she asked the children if there was something special on their wish list. While the older girl pondered her response, the boy rattled off his list. He named all the Saturday morning television toys and ended with a plea for a particular gun.

"I don't give guns for gifts."

"Oh no, grandma, this is just a toy gun," he responded, and began to explain all the marvelous things that this particular toy gun would do.

"I understand that it is just a toy, but I still don't give guns."

"Why? My other grandma buys me guns."

"Well, that's her choice. But I think guns are violent things. They hurt people. Even toy guns are violent." The child frowned.

"Think about what you do when you play with guns. Don't you pretend to shoot and maybe hurt or kill somebody when you point the gun at them?"

"Yeah."

44

"Well, Grandpa and I simply prefer to buy toys that aren't so violent. We know that policemen must carry guns. Sometimes they even have to use them to protect themselves and us. But most of us are better off if we spend our time learning how to live without them. You know, Jimmy, kids learn a lot of things while they play, and Grandpa and I think it's best to play games that help us learn to get along with others. So . . . we don't buy guns, even toy guns."

The little boy shook his head. The discussion had been a bit difficult for him to understand. He could still be heard muttering in the back seat, "My other grandma will buy me the gun."

But his older sister had glimpsed the vision of peace. She cocked her head questioningly and watched the lady driving the car.

"Do you understand what I'm talking about?" asked her grandmother.

Nodding her head, she responded slowly, "Yes, I think I do."

Jesus said, "Blessed are the peacemakers" (Matt. 5:9). We read the words and sometimes help children commit them to memory. But do we help them understand how they can apply the words to their lives? How can we model for children what it means to be a peacemaker?

We might begin by placing a real emphasis on those qualities that go hand-in-hand with peace—justice and respect for others. We might help children discover that peacemaking involves avoiding situations that provoke other persons and nations to violence. Boys and girls can be taught to accept responsibility not only for fighting but also for creating the disturbance and conflict that lead to violence. Because violence often grows out of frustration, children and adults alike must learn to deal with difficulties before tension becomes so bad that conversation is impossible.

The Home—a Laboratory for Peacemaking

If ever there was a laboratory for teaching peace, it is the Christian home. It has the essential ingredients: people and pressures. Parents are under constant pressures—personal disagreements, financial stress, children who spill and fuss and cause sleepless nights when they teethe. Sometimes parents strike out. Sometimes they do not.

The congregation can minister to both children and parents by providing parent training events that address family issues such as discipline. Parents can be challenged to think about the subtleties of name calling. We have heard children referred to (not entirely in jest) as "monsters" and "pests." We have heard adults scream at them as if they were wild animals not deserving of love and respect. Is it any wonder that, in time, some try to prove the labels we give them? Might we look at how children are disciplined, and ask whether striking children is an acceptable way to work out anger and frustration?

The congregation can establish improved parenting skills as a major goal, and through reading, discussion groups, and professional input, assist families with conflict resolution. Children who watch adults manage conflict in nonviolent ways are discovering tools for peacemaking. Nations go to war because they cannot deal creatively and peacefully with conflict!

Parents and teachers constantly search for answers to the question, "What does it mean to be the adult in an adult-child relationship?" We have experimented with answers ranging from authoritarianism to permissiveness—neither of which appears to work well when used to extremes. It seems clear that children need the security of adults who understand that they are adults, not overgrown children, and who will, when necessary, assert their authority, their adultness. Rules, however much resisted, provide security for children; when they are not provided, children fight for the right to establish them.

On the first day of camp one counselor informed the others that he didn't like being a "foster parent" to third and fourth graders. He wanted to be their "friend." The other counselors warned him that these children, most of whom were at camp for the first time, needed the security of his parenting. "I'm going to be their friend," he insisted.

The week passed, and the campers lived peacefully in their living groups—that is, in all but one. The group that did not have an adult willing to be an adult—to be the gatekeeper, to help establish and enforce rules—fought at every opportunity. They called names; they struck out at one another. They were miserable children who were fighting for the right to be the adult.

Even more tragic than the fighting was the fact that they needed to be children. They needed to be loved and protected. They didn't need to be fake adults!

Adults who assert their adultness need not be dictators. Children should have the opportunity to help set their own rules and limits. This experience helps them to grow in their own self-respect, and it helps them to learn the consequences of their choices. But as adults guide

46

children, they are in a position to limit the sometimes overambitious goals of children. They understand that "sooner isn't necessarily better," as well-intentioned as a child's aspirations may be. They can help children look forward to a time in the future when they will be ready to do special things. Generally adults can encourage and guide as they "talk with" children. Sometimes they must, in love, say "no."

"Could you help us with a problem?" asked a mother in a parent training session. "We help our children make the family rules, and sometimes they break them."

"Yes, that happens in families sometimes. What do you want to talk about?"

"We've been trying to decide whether breaking a rule should be punished. You know . . . when should you come down hard on a child, and when do you let it go with a gentle reminder?"

Loving discipline is worth consideration, for it is a way parents and teachers can teach compromise as well as obedience.

Might we counsel with parents and teachers about how children can be taught to respect others and their property? This can usually be done in the course of living and working together. Do parents encourage children to help maintain property by washing table tops and cleaning up their clutter? Do they require children to wipe dirty handprints from the wall or the front of the refrigerator?

A public school teacher tells of giving first graders soap pads and pans of water, then helping them scrub the crayons that they had carelessly mashed into the tile. She did it not to discipline them but to help them understand that their carelessness made unnecessary work for the custodian, who already had a lot to do. Ultimately, she was teaching them an important value in peacemaking, respect for others.

Parents might be encouraged to look carefully at the toys they buy and at the movies and television programs they watch, keeping in mind that war toys and war programs romanticize conflict. When children play constantly with guns and other weapons, they begin to think of them as the ordinary, thus creating an expectancy of war. Some psychologists believe that wars may occur more readily when people expect them and are conditioned to think of them as the best way to solve problems. In this nuclear age, that kind of expectancy spells ultimate disaster for all the world and its children.

Again the importance of unorganized play should be emphasized, for it encourages children to understand something about rules, how they

47

are made and broken, how to manage anger, how to practice the art of peacemaking. Psychologists advise us that children need to learn to live by their *own* rules and experience the consequences of them. Such experiences encourage boys and girls to discover what it means to say, "I'm sorry," and to move on to new and better experiences.

Jesus' parable of the prodigal son (Luke 15:11-32) demonstrates how one person, the younger son, set his own standards, however unwise they may have been, and was allowed to learn from his mistakes. Trial-and-error, however painful, is an effective teacher, particularly when the loving arms of family and friends are ready to offer love and encouragement.

Is it possible for the world to know peace? Many believe it is possible, but all know that it is not easy. Christians and all persons of good will must help others develop a sensitivity for peacemaking in such ways as these:

- Demonstrating a respect for persons of all races and religions. Cross-cultural experiences are important. Parents can help by reading to children stories that depict the worthiness of all people.
- Participating with other concerned people in an effort to provide food for the starving Third World peoples. Obviously this is an important humanitarian gesture, but it also affirms our belief in human dignity and in the value of all life.
- Providing in the home an example of peacemaking by encouraging autonomy in children, de-emphasizing the importance of possessions, helping children learn to forgive, focusing on ways to avoid wasting the earth's resources, and providing peace resources (people, printed materials, pictures, and music).

It has been said that nuclear war is the greatest obscenity of all. Peacemaking must be a clear goal for all of us and for our children. The church must lead the way. Nearly 2,000 years ago, Jesus provided the challenge: "Blessed are the peacemakers."

For Personal Thought and Group Planning

1. Recognizing that only when people are aware that needs exist can they become involved, what new events and/or long-term studies can be planned to raise the consciousness of your church members to issues such as world hunger and peace with justice?

2. What settings can the church provide for teaching peacemaking skills?

3. How might intergenerational events—classes, retreats, game nights, family nights, etc.—encourage communication between members of families and within the faith community?

4. Consider becoming a Peace Advocate in your congregation, particularly with the future of children in mind. For information, contact the Peace Advocate Program, General Board of Discipleship, P.O. Box 840, Nashville, TN 37202.

10 A Ministry without Boundaries.

From time to time we have used the phrase, *ministry without boundaries*. These words may mean different things to different congregations. For instance:

- Christ Church has focused on its own children. For the moment, leaders have all they can do to plan and carry out programs for member families. But they are beginning to talk about needs of children in a nearby housing project.
- First Church has been in ministry to its own children through Sunday school and children's choirs, and to boys and girls in its neighborhood through daycare and after-school care.
- Trinity Church has taken its concern for children into the public school system, providing hundreds of hours each year of volunteer tutoring. Its volunteers also help staff an inner-city kindergarten for Spanish-speaking children.
- Many congregations pool their efforts with those of others to provide workers for a UNICEF walk. They contribute funds to the agencies of the general church that minister to children. They participate actively in work trips to Appalachia, Haiti, or a church in a nearby community.

Ministry without boundaries suggests that people and congregations have limits to ministry beyond which they do not ordinarily go. For each the boundary is different, but more or less traditional. *Yet every boundary can be a frontier!* To bring about changes in the way we usually do things, to move into broader ministries, will require commitment and planning. At some point the question will certainly be asked, "Where do we start?"

Begin by assessing who you are as a congregation, what your financial and personal commitment can be, and what kinds of goals your people are willing and ready to take on. An assessment might look something like this:

1. Who are the children we presently serve?
2. What are we doing to discover the needs of children—our

51

own, children of the community, children of the nation, children of the world?

3. What are we doing to raise the awareness of our membership to the needs of all children?
4. What are we doing to make the congregation aware of the contributions and the concerns of its multi-colored, multi-ethnic community?
5. What can our congregation do to respond to at least one of these identified opportunities?
6. How do we resource these opportunities?
7. With what other agencies, congregations, and persons might we link our energies to plan and implement our goals?
8. What kind of timeline shall we set for ourselves?
9. How do we keep ourselves actively involved in maintaining our awareness of the needs experienced by children?
10. How can we support persons in ministry in the marketplace?

Making It Happen

A huge mound of sand was piled along a main street in Cairo. As the tour bus passed, someone observed, "Look over there. Those men are moving that mound of sand one bucket at a time." My first reaction was to think that it was foolish! Why weren't they using some heavy machinery or, at least, a wheelbarrow?

Later as I remembered the sight, I realized that they were using what they had, and for this, I've developed a respect for those nameless men. It was certainly better for them to do what they could than to sit there wishing the sand were moved. It has been some time since I passed that mountain of sand, and I can't help but believe that the little group of men working together has accomplished its task.

As we plan, we must be realistic. But being realistic about the size of a task does not mean that large tasks should not be addressed. The pile of sand was large, but it was being challenged by simple workmen with the tools, skills, and resources they had available. When churches begin to address issues affecting much of the world's population, they will want to plan realistically, but never losing sight of their dreams.

In an earlier section, it was suggested that a designated leader of children's ministries, often called a coordinator, has a special role in the congregation's program development. In contrast to other leaders, who

52

have a particular assignment related to a program ministry, the coordinator has a concern to share with all of them, a concern for children. What children?

- Those of the congregation. (On many occasions, these will be the primary group served.)
- Those in the community, the city, or the rural area nearby. (These are children you will probably seek out because you have come to understand that there are special needs.)
- Those in the nation and in the world whose special needs should be the concern of your caring congregation.

In every case the children identified and their particular needs can be assigned to one of the program areas of the church and plans developed and implemented there. In fairness to their co-workers, leaders in children's ministry will recognize that these program groups are heavily involved in ministries with all ages—including youth, adults of all ages, and family groupings. It is possible that they may not recognize the urgency of an issue related to children—unless coordinators help them to see it and offer guidance in how issues might be resolved. Let's look at some ways coordinators and other children's leaders might go about their task.

See, Seek, Support.

First suggest that the work areas and other appropriate groups *see* for themselves the needs of children. Offer them your assistance as a resource person and help them to discover the ministry that their area— whether worship, evangelism, stewardship, education, missions, etc. — might offer to children. Go with other leaders if a visit into the community is needed; provide them with resources—articles, surveys, pictures, books, and audiovisuals—to illustrate need.

Offer yourself as one who can link them with others whose expertise or special interest would make them valuable allies or co-workers.

Then *seek* out other agencies in the community with whom you might work. These encounters help to raise the awareness of a wider group of people to specific needs, develop community commitment, increase the probabilities that a project will succeed, and encourage stewardship of time, energy, and resources. Another time it may be you and your congregation who will respond to the invitation of another group to develop a partnership in ministry.

In your role as an advocate for children, *support* other leaders and individuals of the congregation in beginning new programs and sustaining those that are in place. Help people remain aware that special ministries are happening in the lives of children and that prayers and support are needed if these are to continue. Publicize and celebrate your successes. Your support, your advocacy, your celebration will help others to recognize the joy and the importance of our ministries with children.

"What do we call something that is shaped like this?" a teacher asked a group of first graders as she held up a paper plate.

"It's a circle," the children replied.

"Where does the circle begin?" the teacher continued, fully expecting the children's response to prove her point, that there is no beginning and no ending. She fully intended to continue with an explanation that an Advent wreath is shaped like a circle with no beginning and no ending. Then she planned to mention that God's love is like the wreath and the circle. But the children had other ideas.

"At 2:00," they replied brightly, for in their school they were taught to begin their circles at the "2:00" position.

(Later the teacher confessed, "I taught my first graders to begin at 12:00. Things have changed!")

That's where we are as coordinators. We ask ourselves, "Where do we begin?" In each congregation there's structure for ministry. How do we make it work for us?

The wonder is that the work of the coordinator can begin anywhere. The second wonder is that our ministry can go everywhere—anywhere and everywhere. All that is required is that we have a commitment to the God who gave life to all children and cares for each, *and* our own love for children and an interest in what happens to them.

Learn, Envision, Choose, and Act

Remember the symbol of the circle? Place on it the words: *Learn, Envision, Choose,* and *Act.* Add to these words the phrase, *Free to . . ."* As coordinators we are free to envision, free to choose, free to act, and free to learn.

54

FREE TO ENVISION

—To imagine
programs and
settings for ministry
that are new,
different, and
matched to the
needs and hopes of
the people they
seek to serve. We
are free to dream!

FREE TO LEARN

—To acquire through
experience, prayer,
and study the
information,
insights, and ideas
on which to build
new possibilities for
ministry without
boundaries. We are
free to change!

FREE TO CHOOSE

—To select a place or
a group with which
to begin a project
or task that may
not be "business as
usual." We are free
to experiment!

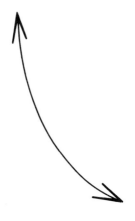

FREE TO ACT

—To enlist others in
efforts to extend
the church's reach
beyond the
boundaries of those
programs and
activities with
which we are most
familiar. We are
free to set our own
course of action!

1. Because we are looking for ways to make the structure work for us, let's begin by thinking about our *freedom to learn*. You have already given time and energy in learning about children, their needs, their concerns, their joys, their fears, and much more. You have probably learned some things about yourself—that you need to study, to seek, to ask, to lift your concerns to God in prayer. You have learned that there is much to discover and there are many resources to enable this discovery.

It isn't long until you discover that learning and the need for new discoveries doesn't stop when you've completed a book or heard a lecture. You have rediscovered something you already knew—that things change, needs and concerns change, strategies for ministry change. Each day the world is a bit different from what it was the day before. Each day children face issues that did not exist in precisely the same way a day or two earlier.

Those planning for ministries with children will include in their plans the elements of flexibility and creativity. They will be ready to receive and accept change when, after deliberation, it is seen as part of a positive move forward. At the same time they will recognize that change for the sake of change is not necessarily in the best interest of children. On the contrary, changes often further the sense of instability which already exists in the lives of many boys and girls.

2. *Freedom to envision* has been a recurring theme in this book as we've thought about helping children learn to dream and to set goals for themselves. But what about the adults who share their lives with children? It's now time for you and all adults who love children to dream about what can happen in the lives of boys and girls if the church makes ministries to them a significant priority. How can we undergird their physical and emotional security? How can we provide security for children who live in a world of uncertainty? How can we involve children in the mission and ministry of the church? How can we help our members and others in the community to become more aware of the plight of hungry children—and challenge them to become involved in doing something about it? How can we enable others to see with us that all children—not just our own—are entitled to dream dreams? What are our dreams for today's children and for those not yet born?

3. *A freedom to choose,* coupled with a special freedom to experiment with new concepts and new approaches to ministry, allows the children's coordinator the luxury of making selections from the long list of concerns related to children. While other council members are work-

ing on the ongoing programs of the church, the coordinator can focus on one, two, or three special needs and issues related to children, and with a particular group, or even with individuals, design events or ministries to deal with them.

Many coordinators are deeply involved in carrying out ongoing ministries. Over the years, this is the way many churches have chosen to use the talents of their coordinators. If this is your situation, take inventory of your investment of time and energy. Can you be freed from some ongoing program responsibilities so as to have time to choose more carefully where your attention and that of the congregation should be directed?

If, in fact, you determine that the direct ministry with children is your task, then explore a realignment of the work load that will free you to dream and to choose from among many dreams. A church will soon discover the creative power of one who is set free to dream and plan.

4. *Freedom to act* suggests an exciting springboard for creative ministries with children. Let us say that in your church the annual Bible school has been an important ministry to the children of the congregation and the community. But attendance has fallen off in the past couple of years, and there are those who are asking if it is worth the work.

In your capacity as coordinator of children's ministries, you've been talking with those who work with children and have discovered an approach that sounds exciting—an intergenerational Bible school to be held in the evenings. Working with the education work area chairperson, you participate as one of a design team to plan and implement this new look in Bible schools.

Someone suggests that a nearby congregation might want to join in the project. Soon it has become a shared ministry to the children and the families of two congregations. Interestingly, the project which you suggested becomes a team experience for your congregation as the family ministries coordinator and several of the work areas join to make it happen. And you have worked through the process—learning, envisioning, choosing, and acting—in your role as coordinator of children's ministries. Now what concern will you address next?

Recall, if you will, the story of the never-beginning, never-ending circle. This time, I would ask you to think of it as a carousel. The first of the four opportunities for coordinators I described was that of *being free to learn*. From there we moved to *envisioning*.

But it doesn't have to work that way. Suppose you first have a dream for children, something like providing a telephone ministry to latchkey children. But it is just a dream at this point; you know little about where to begin. From this point of envisioning you begin to study, to consult with those who know how such a ministry can happen, to research and obtain printed materials. From a dream comes learning. After learning comes action. In other words, you can jump on the carousel at any point, and begin to work.

For Personal Thought and Group Planning

1. Identify five special dreams you have for children in your community and your congregation. Consider some programs and other ministries that would be needed to make these dreams a reality.

2. Prioritize your five dreams, taking into consideration need, availability of resources, persons who share your concern, and other issues that you feel would help to determine your choice of where to begin.

3. Who are the persons or groups to whom you would go for support in planning? In carrying out the plans?

4. What do you need to know before you get deeply involved with planning? Where can you find answers to your questions?

5. What persons share your concern for children? How would you go about inviting them to share their concerns with you?

6. Your "ministry without boundaries" is not limited to programs of the congregation. You have your own ministry as an individual. As a result of this book, what one new individual ministry with children would you now like to take up?

Where Will You Begin?

"What is the greatest crisis facing the world's children today?" a friend asked. The hour-long discussion which followed never did answer the question. Somewhere along the way someone suggested that we were asking the wrong question.

"It's not the children's problem — it's the world's problem." As true as that statement may be, the fact is that problems have to become very personal and relate to someone we know and love before we devote ourselves to looking forward to finding solutions. So . . . while accepting that problems belong to the world, let's think of a child we know and ask the question again.

We made our list of problems, one similar to that suggested earlier. Then we concluded that surely the greatest crisis is the one that each child is experiencing at this very moment: fear, anger, hunger, loneliness—whatever is subverting the child's well-being, the wholeness that God intends for his or her life. We talked about many kinds of needs: starving children; the weak cries of a dying child; the misery of a little boy whose parents are divorcing and who perceives that a life filled with love is gone forever; the pain and struggle of a child on drugs; the tears of children dealing with the death of a loved one—a friend, a parent, or a puppy; children searching for someone they can love who will care for them in the rubble of war; and on and on. These are the places, we concluded, that the church should be in ministry—not instead of, but in addition to our ministry to the children in our homes and congregations.

One of my hopes in writing this book is that many new questions will be raised in your mind. One or two questions will not be enough, for there are many more than one or two issues facing children today. Maybe it is one or two dozen—one or two hundred. The trouble is that when numbers go so high, we are overwhelmed and throw up our hands, crying, "It's no use! There's just too much to be done."

But we are unwilling, aren't we, to give up—to let the hunger, the disease, the wars, the ugliness destroy us and the children we love. It is true that we don't have all the answers, but we do have some of them.

We know that if a child-care facility is what we need for our community, there are government and church agencies that will help us get started.

We know that if we want to start an emergency phone service for latchkey children, our own United Methodist Board of Discipleship has resources to guide us.

We know that if we want to concentrate on hungry children in Africa, South America, or the United States, the church has agencies and resources to focus our energies.

There is another step, one I believe to be crucial. It has been suggested earlier in terms of helping children become imaginative Christians and citizens of the world. Judy Gattis Smith tells of a day when she took a group of fifth and sixth grade boys and girls outside and invited them to stretch out on their backs and look at the sky. Lying there in the grass, she asked them to commit to memory a very short Bible verse: "Be still and know that I am God."

If you cannot, right now, do as those children did, then use your imagination. Close your eyes for a little while, then look with your mind's eye into the billowing clouds. Acknowledge who you are and whose you are. Acknowledge that God is speaking today—challenging the church to be the church, to serve children. What does this call mean to you? What needs do you perceive? What new ministries do you begin to imagine? Where will you begin?

Learn. Envision. Choose. And *act!*

Resources

The following resources will be useful in further thought and planning for a children's ministry without boundaries. Except as indicated, resources may be ordered from Discipleship Resources, P.O. Box 189, Nashville, TN 37202.

Guidelines for Leadership in the Local Church: 1985-88: Children's Ministries (Abingdon Press). The basic guide for the local church coordinator of children's ministries and others with general responsibility in this area. Relationships, responsibilities, tasks, and planning for the year.

Leaders Make a Difference! Skills for Members of the Administrative Council, Administrative Board and Council on Ministries by Cherie Parker (Discipleship Resources). Leader's Guide and four handouts for a four-session workshop to help leaders see the congregation's ministry in terms of a vision for their community.

We Don't Have Any Here (Discipleship Resources). Examples and principles for the congregation's ministry with persons with handicapping conditions in the community.

We Can Break the Cycle of Child Abuse: An Adult Study (Discipleship Resources). In this book Virginia Kent helps us understand the scope of child abuse and neglect, some of the causes, and the kinds of help available. Suggested decisions and actions for readers who want to help, individually or through groups.

I've Got Something to Share! by Susan A. Patterson-Sumwalt (Discipleship Resources). A six-session children's stewardship unit (grades three through six). *Leader's Guide* and *Student Leaflets.*

God Made Us: About Sex and Growing Up (Graded Press). Helps for planning and leading a six-session study of sexuality for children grades three through six, with related sessions for parents. *Student's Book* and *Leader's Guide.* (Order from Cokesbury, P.O. Box 801, Nashville, TN 37202.)

The Child Advocacy Handbook (Pilgrim Press). A focus on action, not theory. This is an indispensable resource for anyone who wants to insure basic care, love, and opportunity for all children. By Happy Craven Fernandez.

The Children, Yes! (Discipleship Resources). A timely and comprehensive resource for understanding and involving children in your congregation's worship, by Phillip McLarty.

Communion Book for Children (Discipleship Resources). For use by children during Sunday worship. Full-color art and photographs illustrate the movement through the service of the Word and the Service of Holy Communion. By Diedra Kriewald and Barbara García.

How to Teach Peace to Children (Herald Press). J. Lorne Peachy surveys what has been written in Mennonite, Brethren, and Quaker publications since World War II on how parents can pass peace values on to children. Twenty-one specific ideas.

Children and Worship Resources Packet (Discipleship Resources). Includes four leaflets: *Worship Guides for Children, Keep Them in Their Place?, Worship Readiness,* and *Preparing Parents and the Congregation for the Baptism of Infants and Children.*